Genesis Anthology, Volume 1.

Wise Publications.
London/New York/Sydney/Cologne

Exclusive Distributors:
Music Sales Limited,
78 Newman Street, London W1P 3LA, England.
Music Sales Pty. Limited,
27 Clarendon Street, Artarmon, Sydney, NSW 2064, Australia.

This book © Copyright 1985 by
Wise Publications
ISBN 0.7119.0698.X
Order No. AM39918

Design by Pearce Marchbank Studio.
Cover photography by L.F.I.
Music compiled by Peter Evans.

Music Sales complete catalogue lists thousands of
titles and is free from your local music book shop,
or direct from Music Sales Limited.
Please send 25p in stamps for postage to
Music Sales Limited, 78 Newman Street, London W1P 3LA.

Printed in England by
The Camelot Press Limited, Southampton.

The Lamb Lies Down On Broadway.

Tony Banks, Phil Collins, Mike Rutherford, Peter Gabriel and Steve Hackett.

© Copyright 1974 Genesis Music Ltd.
Hit & Run Music (Publishing) Ltd., 81/83 Walton Street, London SW3.
All Rights Reserved. International Copyright Secured.

on the land.___ The Mov-ie Pal-ace is now un-done.___ The
down the chains.___ Met-al mo-tion comes in bursts,___ but the
be on, ne-on.___ Cab-man's vel-vet glove sounds the horn,___ and the

all-night watch-men have had their fun.___ Sleep-ing cheap-ly on the
gas sta-tion___ can quench that thirst.___ Sus-pen-sion cracked___ on
saw-dust king___ spits out his scorn.___ Won-der wom-en,

mid-night show,___ it's the same old end-ing; time to go.___ Get out!___
un-made road.___ The truck-er's eyes___ read "o-ver-load."___
draw your blind!___ Look at me!___ I'm not your kind.___ I'm real!___

on Broad - way.

Broad - way.

The lamb seems right out of place, yet the Broad - way street

scene finds a fo - cus in its face. Some-how it's ly - ing

I Know What I Like (In Your Wardrobe).

Tony Banks, Phil Collins, Mike Rutherford, Peter Gabriel and Steve Hackett.

(spoken) *It's one o'clock and time for lunch.*

When the sun beats down and I lie on the bench, I can always hear them talk.

There's al - ways been Eth - el:

"Ja - cob, wake up. You've got to ti - dy your room now."

And then Mis - ter Lew - is: "Is-n't it time that he was out on his own?"

O - ver the gar - den wall, two lit - tle love - birds cuck - oo to you.

Keep them mow - ing blades sharp. I know what I like, and I

like what I know: get - ting bet - ter in your

ward-robe, step-ping one be-yond_ your show._

_ Sun-day night,_ Mis - ter Farm - er called, said,

"Lis-ten, son,_ you're wast - ing time._There's a fu-ture for you_ in the fire_ es-cape trade.

Come up to town." But I re - mem-bered a voice_ from the past:_

"Gam-bling on-ly pays_when you're win-ning." I had to thank old Miss Mort_ for school-ing a fail-

D. S. %al Coda ⊕

Coda

A

ure. Keep them mow-ing blades sharp. I

(spoken) When the

A

sun beats down and I lie on the bench, I can always hear them talk. Me, I'm just a lawnmower. You can

Repeat and fade

A

tell me by the way I walk.

Carpet Crawl.

Peter Gabriel, Mike Rutherford, Steve Hackett, Phil Collins and Tony Banks.

life - blood than be - fore. They're mov - ing ___ in time to a

D   Em

heav - y wood-en door ___ where the eag - le's eye is wink-ing clos - ing

D   Em

𝄋 CHORUS

___ on the poor. ___ The Car - pet crawl - ers ___ heed their call -

F♯m7

- ers ___ you've got to get in ___ to get out. ___

A(sus4)   A   G

get in ____ to get out ____   get out, ____ get out, ____ know, know,

Em

____ know,   know, ____ you've got to ____ get out. ____

D. S. al Coda

Em

⊕ *CODA*

D   D

Verse 2

    There's only one direction in the faces that I see
    And it's upward to that ceiling where the chamber's said to be.
    Like the forest fight for sunlight that takes root in every tree
    They are pulled up by the magnet still believing they are free.
            (to chorus)

Verse 3

    Mild mannered supermen are held in kryptonite,
    And wise & foolish virgins giggle with their bodies glowing bright.
    And through the door a harvest feast is lit by candlelight,
    It's the bottom of a staircase that spirals out of sight.
            (to chorus)

Verse 4

    The porcelain mannikin .with shattered skin fears his next attack,
    The eager pack lift up their pitchers they carry on their back
    The liquid has congealed which has seeped out through the crack,
    And the tickler takes his stickle back,—back, back, back, back, back, back.
            (to chorus)

Firth Of Fifth.

Peter Gabriel, Mike Rutherford, Steve Hackett, Phil Collins and Tony Banks.

1: The path is clear though no eyes can see The
2: He rides ma-jes - tic past homes of men Who

B   A⁶₉   E/G♯   B

[4th time]

course laid down long be - fore.
care not or gaze with joy.

Em/G♮   F♯m7   F♯7 B(sus4)   B7

And so, with gods__ and men   the sheep re-main in-side__ their pen,__ Though
To see re-flec - ted there,   the trees, the sky, the lil - y fair,__ The

E   F♯m7/E   Bm/D   Cmaj7/D

ma - ny times they've seen   the way   to leave.
scene of death   is ly - ing just be-low.

G   E   B♭dim

The moun - tain   cuts off   the town   from

E   A   Emaj7

view   Like a can - cer growth   is re - moved   by

A   B♭m   E♭m   B♭7

19

skill. Let it be re - vealed.   A

wa - ter-fall,   his mad - ri - gal,   An

in - land sea,   his sym - pho - ny.

Eb   Eb/F   F   G

Bb/C   Cm/F

E6   B   E6

B   C#m7/F#

20

3: Now as the river dissolves in sea,
   So Neptune has claimed another soul.
   And so, with gods and men, the sheep remain inside their pen
   Until the shepherd leads his flock away.

4: The sands of time were eroded by
   The river of constant change.

A Trick Of The Tail.

Tony Banks.

down the door of the cage and marched on out. ___ He

grabbed a crea - ture by the scruff of his neck, ___ point-ing out: ___

"There, be - yond   the bounds ___   of your

weak i-mag-i - na - tion   lie the no-ble tow - ers of my

25

Afterglow.

Tony Banks.

Like the dust ___ that set-tles all a - round ___ me,
than the sun ___ re - flect-ing off my pil - low,

The mean-ing of all __ that I __ be-lieved __ be-fore __ es-

capes me __ in this world __ of none. __ I miss __ you more. __

Repeat and fade

Ripples.

Mike Rutherford and Tony Banks.

Follow You Follow Me.

Tony Banks, Phil Collins and Mike Rutherford.

41

42

Entangled.

Steve Hackett and Tony Banks.

When you're a-sleep they may show you — aer-i-al views of the ground, Freud-i-an slum-bers emp-ty of

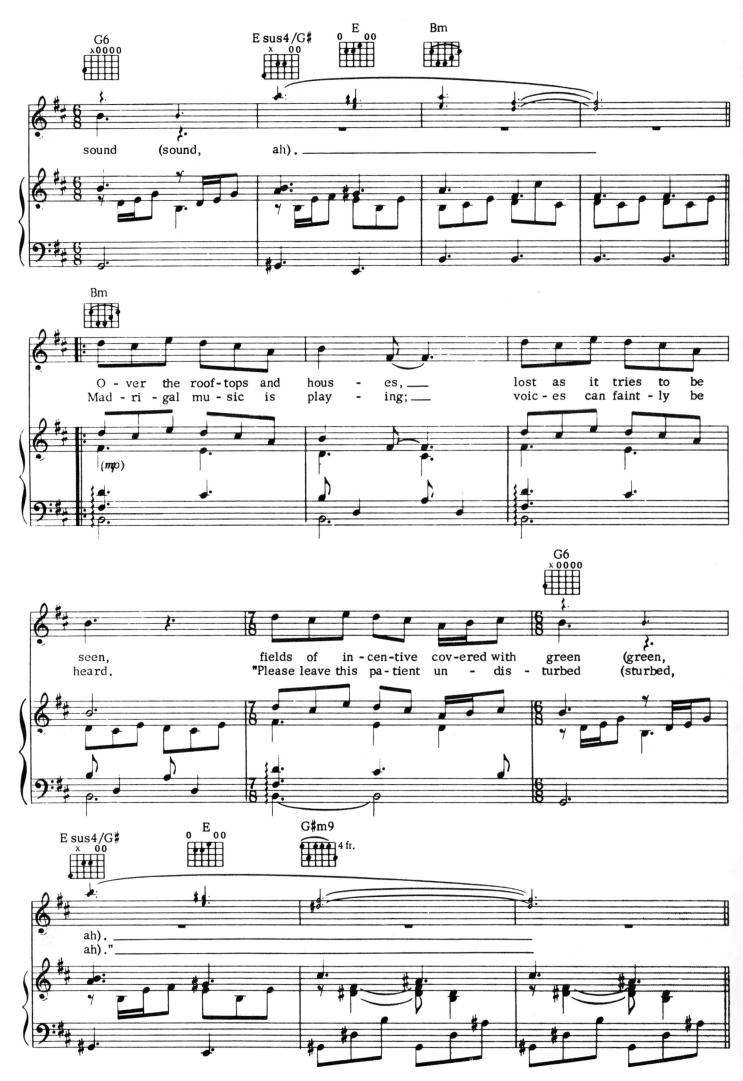

sound (sound, ah). _____

O - ver the roof-tops and hous - es, ___ lost as it tries to be
Mad - ri - gal mu - sic is play - ing; ___ voic - es can faint - ly be

seen, fields of in - cen-tive cov-ered with green (green,
heard. "Please leave this pa - tient un - dis - turbed (sturbed,

ah). _____
ah)."

With your con - sent I can   ex - per - i - ment fur - ther
you catch your breath and the   nurse will pre - sent you the

all.
til

still."
bill."

Undertow.

Tony Banks.

out there __ And some there are
our doubts __ And soon we are feel

cold, they pre-pare for a sleep-less night, may-be this will be their
why do a sin-gle thing to-day, there's to-mor-row sure as

last fight. __ But we're safe in each oth-er's em-
I'm here. __ So the days they turn in-to __

-brace All fears go as I look in your face.
years And still no to-mor-row ap-pears.

Bet-ter

49

Let me feel once more the arms__ of love sur - round__ me

tell - ing me__ the dan - ger's past,__ I need not fear the ic - y blast a -

gain.

Ballad Of Big.

Tony Banks, Phil Collins and Mike Rutherford.

still won't lie down   For him the

bet is still on,   some say he rides there __   curs - ing

still,   some say they've seen him. __

Repeat and fade ad lib.

57

Snowbound.

Mike Rutherford.

Lay your bo - dy down ___ up - on the mid - night snow, ___
Smil - ing fac - es tear your bo - dy to the ground ___

Feel the cold of win - ter in your hair.
Cov - ered red that on - ly we can see. ___

Pray
Hey!   for the snow-man.
        there lies the snow-man.

Ooh!   Ooh!_____
Hey!_____ he was a snow-man.

What a snow-man.

They say a snow year's a good year filled with the love of___

___ all___ who lie so deep.___lie so___ deep.___

1 only   D.C. 2 (and for repeat to fade)

D.S. (repeat Chorus
ad lib. to fade)

61

Your Own Special Way.

Mike Rutherford.

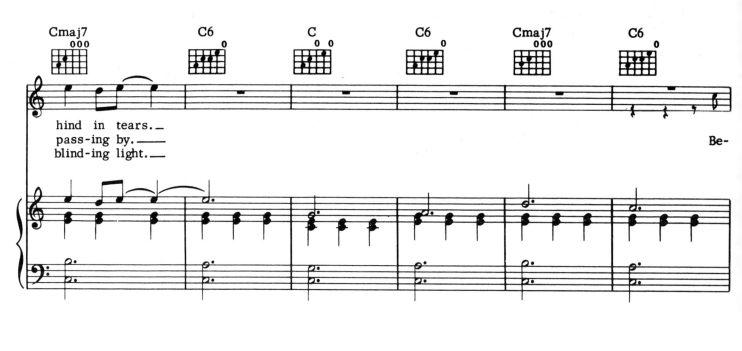

hind in tears.
pass-ing by.
blind-ing light.

Be-

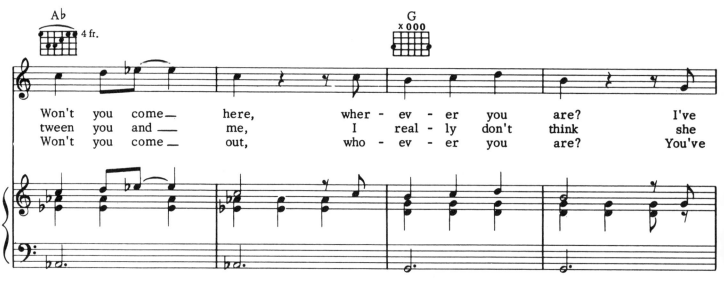

Won't you come here, wher - ev - er you are? I've
tween you and me, I real - ly don't think she
Won't you come out, who - ev - er you are? You've

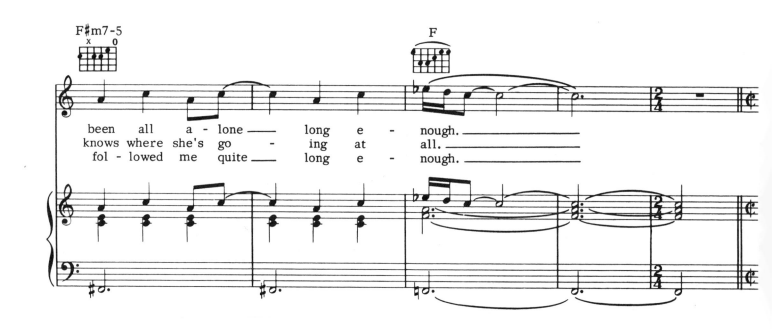

been all a - lone long e - nough.
knows where she's go - ing at all.
fol - lowed me quite long e - nough.

Blood On The Rooftops.

Steve Hackett and Phil Collins.

Moderately

Dark and grey, an Eng-lish film, the Wednes - day Play. We
Hyp - no - tised by Bat - man, Tar - zan; still sur - prised! You've

al - ways watch the Queen on Christ-mas day. Won't you stay?
won the West in time to be our guest. Name your prize!

Dance On A Volcano.

Mike Rutherford, Tony Banks, Steve Hackett and Phil Collins.

Ho - ly Moth - er of
half - way up ___ and you're
mu - sic's play - ing; the

God, you've got ___ to go fast - er than that ___ to get to the top. ___
half - way down, __ and the pack on your back __ is turn-ing you a - round.
notes are right.. Put your left foot first, and ___ move in - to the light. ___ The

On your left ___ and on your right, ___ cross-es are green ___ and cross-es are blue. ___ Your friends did-n't make ___ it through. ___

blaz - ing hot, the mol - ten rock spills out o - ver the

land.

And the

la-va's the lov - er who licks your boots a - way.

Hey, hey,

hey.

If you don't want to boil as well, ___

80

Down And Out.

Tony Banks, Phil Collins and Mike Rutherford.

1: It's good to be here! How've you
2: I need a shower, take a
3: *See block lyric*

VERSE 3

The drinks are on me, — be my guest —
Smoke a cigar? — Take the best.
Don't hedge your bets, we can make a deal,
Got it in your pocket? — How d'you feel?
So glad that's over — now you know
But I'm only acting under orders.
And looking down on you from way up here
You've got to sink or swim, — get off the floor!
(to Chorus)

Deep In The Motherlode.

Mike Rutherford.

Get out-a the way, fat_man you got some-thing to do. Go fill up your hands___

till they're shin - ing_ up at_ you. ___

You got-ta get out while there's gold in the air. It's fall-ing like wat-er

com-ing down from the hills.

Go west, young man
Go west, young man

earn a dol-lar a day.
if you knew then

87

So go west, young man,

go west, young man, like your fam - il - y said.

91

Many Too Many.

Tony Banks.

1: Ma- ny, too ma - ny, have stood where I stand

2: The past was fun ___ but now it's ov - er.

Man - y more will stand here too ____

Why can't I ____ just leave the stage ____

VERSE 3

You said goodbye on a corner
that I thought led to the straight,
You set me on a firmly laid and simple course
and then removed the road.

    Oh Mama — please help me find my way.
    Oh pretty Mama, please lead me throught the next day.

I thought I was lucky
I thought that I'd got it made
—how could I be so blind?

Squonk.

Mike Rutherford and Tony Banks.

All are not hunts - men who can blow ___ the hunts - man's horn. By the look of this ___

___ one, you've ___ not ___ got much to fear. ___

Here I am; I'm ver - y fierce and fright-'ning.

Come to match my ___ skill to yours. ___ Now

All in all,—you are—a ver-y dy - ing race,— plac-ing trust up-on— a cru-

el world.— You nev-er had the things— you thought— you should have had, — and

you'll not get — them now.— And all the while — in per - fect time,— your tears are fall-

ing on — the ground. -

gradual decresc.

105

Misunderstanding.

Phil Collins.

and you were late.＿　　　　　Now, it's

not like me to say the right ＿ thing,　　　　but you
must be some mis-un-der-stand-ing.　　　　There

could have called ＿ to let me know. ＿　　　　I
must be some ＿ kind of mis-take. ＿　　　　I

checked your num-ber twice. ＿ Don't un-der-stand ＿ it.　　　So I went home. ＿
wait-ed in the rain ＿ for hours, ＿　　　and you were late. ＿

Turn It On Again.

Tony Banks, Phil Collins and Mike Rutherford.

luck a - gain. Down on my luck a - gain.
oth - er day, and we will fly a - way?

I can show you, I can show you some of the peo - ple in my

life. I can show you, I can show you

some of the peo - ple in my life. It's driv - in' me mad.

111

113

Heathaze.

Tony Banks.

Please Don't Ask.

Phil Collins.

Cul-De-Sac.

Tony Banks.

and don't spare the los - er.

los - er now.

Now the host _ e - merg - es. A shad -

don't e - ven know he's there?___ And now that the time ___ is al -

most done,___ may - be some es - cape.___ No, ___ not e - ven

one.

D. S. ℀ al Coda ⊕

Coda

los - er.